The Franchise Leap

Franchise Your Business, Become A Successful Investor And Experience Massive Growth

Jeremy J. Holland

Table Of Contents

INTRODUCTION

Try not to be tricked into thinking you need to begin a business without any preparation to be an entrepreneur, or that you're not a business person except if you go solo. That is gibberish. Being a franchising proprietor is one of the best ways of accomplishing business possession and fulfilling your innovative soul.

Meaning Of Franchising

A franchise is a plan where the proprietor of the brand and plan of action gives you the option to utilise said brand and plan of action (with all going to brand names, items, frameworks, and so on) in return for cash. In the establishment framework, the proprietor is the franchisor and you are the franchisee.

This is the manner by which a franchise becomes: a business person begins a free private venture, and over the long haul refines it into an effective and stable plan of action. How about we call this business visionary Alex. Alex understands the adequacy of what she has constructed, and needs to extend it. She could do this by opening more branches herself, or she could sell her plan of action (and all going to advantages) to another business person.

Sam needs to work for himself, however doesn't be guaranteed to manage the experimentation of going into business without any preparation. He needs to utilise someone's plan of action that has previously been demonstrated, with a brand that has far and wide acknowledgment. Sam can buy Alex's image and plan of action. Sam then, at that point, opens an establishment area and maintains his business as per the model Alex created. He will utilise a market-tried brand, showcasing materials, plan of action, procedures and items. In this present circumstance, a franchise understanding is a shared benefit for both Alex and Sam. Alex will create her image and financial momentum by growing through a franchisee, and Sam will turn into his own manager with a demonstrated plan of action (and without the gamble and obscureness that can accompany a startup).

For the utilisation of her image, Sam pays Alex some type of a one-time franchise charge, and ordinarily a yearly level of income as a sovereignty.

The Difference Between Franchising, Chains and Permitting

How does diversifying vary from a chain or authorised business? The ideas are comparable, however each has explicit qualifiers that hold it separated.

A chain is a gathering of indistinguishable organisations that utilise similar logos, items, showcasing, and so on (very much like a franchise) where every individual area is possessed by the parent. This implies that an area can have a senior supervisor who runs everyday tasks, except that individual doesn't claim the business. With an establishment, as we probably are aware, every area is claimed by the person.

Eateries are the most well-known type of this, however not by any means the only choice. Costco and Walmart are chains: different areas, each claimed by Costco or Walmart's focal business structure.

An authorised store has somewhat more unobtrusive contrasts. It is basically the same as franchise in that the brand proprietor (licensor) allows the individual (licensee — are you detecting a subject here?) for the brand to be utilised and items to be sold, yet the construction and charges related contrast broadly. Regularly, the licensor has practically no functional control of the licensee, and the licensee gets fundamentally less preparation from the brand. Moreover, there is ordinarily nobody time expense forthright, as with a franchise. All things considered, a progressing authorising charge is normally evaluated.

A fantastic illustration of authorised stores are Starbucks that show up within different stores, similar to an Objective or Safeway, frequently as a major booth as opposed to an independent space. These little Starbucks actually convey each of similar espressos, and products, however they are not held to similar norms as conventional Starbucks areas. Nor are the Objective Starbucks baristas workers of Starbucks: they're utilised by Target.

The Upsides and downsides of Franchise Possession

Normally, all business valuable open doors have their advantages and disadvantages. For your purposes, a portion of these cons might be advantages, as well as the other way around.

Stars

- **Demonstrated plan of action**: Alex has proactively gone through months or long stretches of experimentation to refine her plan of action. Frequently, being a franchisee eliminates a large part of the gamble built into a startup, on the grounds that the franchisor has previously committed errors. You get to procure the information from those errors without making them yourselves. (Obviously, any kind of business conveys risk, franchise included. Franchise is not a supernatural, achievement guaranteed venture.)

• **Market-tried items or administrations**: The item or administration has proactively gotten input from the market — it's now gone through the initial not many rounds of intense test time. Furthermore, once more, you get to receive the benefits of those errors without paying for them yourself.

• **Memorability**: One of the most troublesome parts of maintaining a private venture is getting clients the entryway. With a franchise, the brand is much of the time currently broadly conspicuous. One clear model is Tram. Or on the other hand a later model is Menchies. Your franchisor has previously attempted to fabricate the brand you'll utilise so you don't need to.

- **Domain security**: At the point when you buy a franchise area, you likewise get a particular geographic domain. This implies your franchisor won't sell another establishment area excessively near yours — they don't need their franchisees contending with each other for a piece of the pie, and neither do you. You might buy various domains without a moment's delay, to grow your number of areas.

- **Promoting support**: Alongside memorability, the franchisor will frequently promote trademarks, pictures, content and backing with building your procedures and spending plan. Some franchisors even have public or global advertising efforts that they run for the benefit of their areas.

- **Preparing program**: Preparing programs are run of the mill incorporated into a franchise framework to provide you with a strong comprehension of the plan of action and techniques for running an area.

• **Functional help**: Numerous franchisors have a group committed to progressing support for yourself as well as your area. They'll address your inquiries and help with the many subtleties that accompany their establishment image.

• **Underlying emotionally supportive network**: To wrap things up, being a franchisee implies you have an underlying emotionally supportive network of other franchisees. The brand will have online discussions and yearly shows where franchisees can meet up, answer questions, exchange tips and deceives, and so on.

Cons

• **Rules and guidelines**: There are explicit standards around how, when and where to work your franchise area. They limit the franchisor's opportunity to do anything that the individual in question wishes.

• **Expenses and eminences**: Buying your area can be costly — much more so than purchasing a free business or building your own. Franchisees likewise regularly owe a level of income back to the franchisor as a sovereignty.

• **High beginning up costs**: Beyond the establishment expense, the expense of really getting your entryways open can be exceptionally high. Normally, a franchisee is expected to get hardware and materials through the franchisor. This can periodically be more costly than if the franchisee had the opportunity to pick an alternate provider.

CHAPTER 1

Understanding Franchising

At its centre, a franchise is a business game plan where one party, known as the franchisor, awards another party, known as the franchisee, the option to work a business utilising its laid out brand, frameworks, and cycles.

This plan permits the franchisee to use the standing and acknowledgment of the franchisor's image, profiting from the trust and dependability previously settled by the franchisor on the lookout. When a franchisee buys a franchise, they are basically putting resources into a demonstrated plan of action. This implies that they don't need to begin without any preparation and sort out each part of maintaining an effective business. All things being equal, they get sufficiently close to an exhaustive arrangement of rules, systems, and procedures that have proactively been tried and refined by the franchisor.

This help can incorporate help with site choice, advertising efforts, functional direction, and ceaseless preparation programs. By getting this help, franchisees can explore the difficulties of beginning and growing a business fully supported by experienced experts.

Key Components of a Franchise

An effective franchise requires a few critical components to flourish. First and foremost, there should be a clear cut brand and business idea that has been shown to find success. A solid brand draws in clients and separates the franchise . This help can take different structures, for example, ordinary correspondence, field visits, preparing projects, and admittance to an organisation of individual franchisees. The franchisor's obligation to support their franchisees is critical in keeping up with the general outcome of the franchise framework. Besides, a franchise understanding, an authoritative record framing the freedoms as well as expectations of the two players, is a necessary piece of any franchise. It covers regions, for example, expenses, an area, licensed innovation privileges, and end conditions.

Franchise Agreement

A franchise agreement is a lawfully authoritative agreement that frames the privileges, commitments, and assumptions for both the franchisor and franchisee. This arrangement fills in as the franchise for the franchisor-franchisee relationship and covers different fundamental parts of the establishment business.

One critical component tended to in the franchise agreement is the domain. The arrangement determines the geographic region wherein the franchisee has the select right to work the franchise. This guarantees that the franchisor doesn't allow extra franchise in a similar region, which might actually prompt contest between franchisees.

One more basic angle canvassed in the franchise agreement is the charges. The arrangement frames the underlying establishment charge, which is the forthright instalment made by the franchisee to the franchisor for the option to work the franchise. Furthermore, it might incorporate continuous sovereignty expenses, showcasing charges, and other monetary commitments that the franchisee should satisfy all through the span of the arrangement.

Licensed innovation freedoms are additionally tended to in the franchise arrangement.

Moreover, the franchise arrangement incorporates end statements that frame the conditions under which either party can end the understanding. These conditions safeguard both the franchisor and franchisee in the event of breaks, rebelliousness, or other unanticipated conditions.

Given the intricacy and lawful ramifications of a franchise agreement, it is fundamental for the two players to counsel legitimate experts experienced in diversifying. These experts can guarantee that the arrangement is fair, adjusted, and good for both the franchisor and franchisee, decreasing the gamble of likely debates or lawful issues from here on out.

The Franchise Disclosure Document(FDD)

The franchisor is lawfully expected to furnish the franchisee with a Franchise Disclosure Document (FDD) before the franchisee consents to any limiting arrangements or commits any monetary responsibilities.The

FDD commonly incorporates the accompanying segments:

1. Franchisor's Experience: This segment gives data about the franchisor's set of experiences, insight, and key work force. It helps the franchisee survey the franchisor's believability and history.

2. Franchisee Commitments: This segment frames the obligations and commitments of the franchisee, including functional prerequisites, preparing, and continuous help gave by the franchisor.

3. Introductory and Continuous Expenses: Here, the FDD subtleties the underlying venture expected to begin the franchise, including franchise charges, hardware costs, and different costs. It likewise takes care of progressing expenses like sovereignties, publicising charges, and some other monetary commitments.

4. Monetary Execution: This segment gives verifiable monetary data about the franchise framework, including marketing projections, benefit, and other significant monetary information.

5. Legitimate and Case History: The FDD unveils any past or progressing legitimate questions including the franchisor, like claims or administrative activities. It is prescribed to look for proficient exhortation, for example, talking with a franchise lawyer or bookkeeper, to guarantee a far-reaching comprehension of the FDD and its suggestions.

Taking everything into account, understanding the lawful parts of franchising is fundamental for both franchisors and franchisees. The franchise understanding and Franchise Disclosure Document act as essential devices in laying out a fair and commonly useful franchisor-franchisee relationship.

Looking for legitimate direction and leading an exhaustive reasonable level of effort prior to going into a franchise understanding can assist with relieving dangers and set the franchise for a fruitful franchise venture.

CHAPTER 2

Franchising- A Strategy For Business Growth

Following quite a while of working a fruitful private venture, business people frequently wind up at an intersection on the most proficient method to successfully grow their organisation while limiting gambling. When your image has demonstrated its plan of action is concrete, and you have a faithful client base, the following coherent step is to grow your organisation's presence.

Taking your business to the following period of its prosperity and entering new business sectors, be that as it may, can come for an extreme price. Notwithstanding the capital expected to foster your business, proprietors should likewise calculate the staff to scale activities to address the issues of the new business sectors they're endeavouring to reach.

At the point when you wind up at such an intersection, diversifying your business idea might be a superb choice for you. Diversifying is a critical technique to assist with expanding a business' piece of the pie. It's viewed as by numerous a definite fire way for a fruitful business to stretch out without having to finance its own extension straightforwardly.

Two of the most engaging parts of diversifying are that it permits an organisation the capacity to rapidly scale while limiting gambling and that it takes out the need to raise extreme capital or increment above.

While diversifying is a proficient instrument for organisations, it's likewise a rewarding business opportunity for yearning and prepared business people. Diversifying gives individuals the chance to maintain their own business with the help and direction of a bigger organisation with a demonstrated limit.

- **Diversifying can help you restrict and broaden activities.**

Diversifying gives an organisation the chance to be neighbourhood yet versatile and reliable. This kind of development is hard to accomplish as a corporate substance alone.

New franchise proprietors hoping to open an area in their specific local area or market frequently have a profound comprehension of the necessities and feelings of that local area. By venturing into new domains and districts through diversifying, your organisation's administrations are made accessible to a more extensive crowd, both expanding and limiting your compass.

• Risk in diversifying is generally low.

Opening an independent business or a franchise is no simple accomplishment. However, diversifying an idea decreases a ton of the gamble that goes into building or growing a business without any preparation — for both the franchisor and franchisee. With diversification, the franchisor can go through the scaling system of their business without forfeiting the nature of their administrations, raising outside assets or incrementing above costs. On the opposite side, franchisees benefit from entering an all around demonstrated plan of action with set up assets behind it. Obviously, opening a franchise isn't something you can embrace for the time being. Yet, diversifying as opposed to beginning a business from the starting point can offer entrepreneurs a platform as well as an emotionally supportive network to get everything rolling.

• Franchisor-franchisee connections are critical.

Franchisors ordinarily give the preparation proprietors need to work inside the franchise's plan of action. Many likewise give showcasing backing and mentorship and don't need a degree or mastery in a specific field to begin. Truth be told, franchises have a higher pace of progress than new companies. As per a review conducted by FranNet, 85% of franchisees stay in business for a considerable length of time or longer. Contrast this with a report by Investopedia showing that just around half of new businesses most recent five years or longer.

• Diversifying gives open doors to development in pieces of the pie.

Diversifying your idea can likewise assist with smoothing out your business' cycles and increment generally a piece of the pie so your organisation can offer more administrations to bigger socioeconomics of individuals.

CHAPTER 3

Benefits Of Franchising Your Business For Growth

1. Quick Development with Lower Capital Consumption: Diversifying permits organisations to extend without the weighty monetary weight of buying and working various outlets themselves. All things being equal, individual franchisees put resources into setting up their areas. This model methods the essential business causes insignificant capital use, yet partakes in the upside of a more extensive market presence. Collaborating with a franchise improvement organisation can additionally smooth out this cycle, guaranteeing each step lines up with the brand's overall development methodology.

2. Consistency in Brand Picture and Administrations: One of the eminent franchise benefits is the consistency it brings. While every outlet could have an alternate proprietor, the brand picture, administration quality, and client experience stay reliable. This consistency is basically guaranteed through fastidious documentation and preparation gave to franchisees.

3. Expanded Income Streams: Past the income from the centre business activities, franchising presents valuable pay sources. These come through franchising charges, continuous sovereignties, and potential mass stockpile concurrences with franchisees.

4. Hearty Market Entrance: Each franchisee brings nearby market information, experiences, and associations. This nearby ability, joined with the brand's laid out standing, works with more profound market entrance. Franchise marketing specialists assume an essential part in this viewpoint, planning on the most proficient method to use nearby experiences while keeping up with worldwide brand information. Compelling franchise marketing guarantees that the brand stays top-of-mind for buyers across locales.

5. Shared Hazard: Franchising intrinsically isolates the business risk. Since franchisees put resources into their outlets, they share the functional and market gambles with the essential brand. This chance appropriation can make it more straightforward for the parent organisation to explore different avenues regarding new market methodologies or items, realising that not all dangers are carried by the organisation alone.

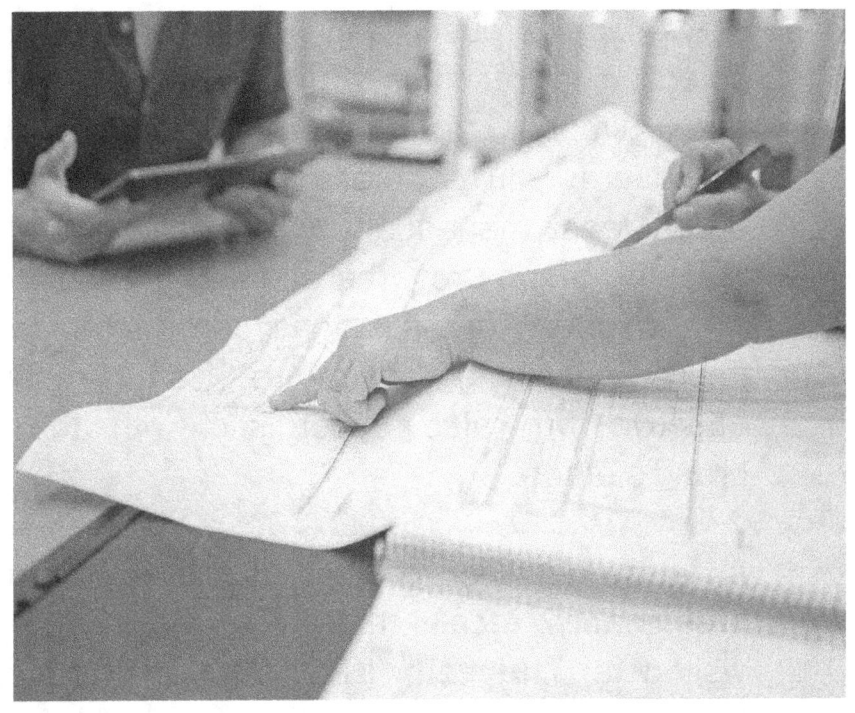

6. Persistent Input for Development: With various franchisees working in fluctuated markets, the parent organisation benefits from a consistent criticism circle. Drawing in with a franchise consulting organisation can additionally help in grouping, breaking down, and coordinating this criticism into the business system, guaranteeing the brand stays dexterous and client-driven. By selecting to franchise your business, you're not simply picking a development procedure; you're embracing a model that guarantees manageability, versatility, and reliable brand reverberation. By utilising their mastery, organisations can guarantee their franchising adventure isn't simply effective but also synergistic with their brand's ethos.

A larger number of times than you can presumably recall that, you've probably visited a 7-Eleven, KFC, McDonald's or Dunkin' to partake in the comfort and administrations of a brand you know and trust. Their proprietors put resources into a realised brand in order to make business progress.

As an entrepreneur, you continually seek after techniques to extend and develop your image. One down to earth approach for achieving this objective is through franchising. By banding together with people who are curious in buying and working their own organisations, you can expand your image's range and lift your income. By franchising your image, you can grow your compass and increment your income without assuming the whole weight of opening and dealing with various areas independently. With each new franchisee, you can produce extra pay through starting franchise fees, ongoing royalty payments, and other monetary plans. With regards to developing your business through franchising, you won't be separated from everyone else all the while. There are a large number of help and assets accessible to help you en route.

Franchise affiliations, career expos, and meetings give important systems administration open doors and instructive assets. Banks and moneylenders additionally have explicit supporting choices for franchise businesses. With reasonable sponsorship and assets, you can unhesitatingly explore the franchising venture and guarantee the progress of your image.

CHAPTER 4

Choosing The Right Franchise

Assuming that you're thinking about diversifying, check the below options to guarantee you pick the best and open the door for your necessities, objectives and financial plan.

1. Pinpoint your franchise inclinations and necessities: Similarly as with beginning a vocation or starting any new business, you should comprehend your inclinations and requirements while investigating diversifying.

2. Research organisations offer diversifying open doors: When you comprehend the boundaries you'll require in your diversifying excursion and know your favoured industry, now is the ideal time to explore organisations with diversifying open doors that fit the bill. Begin by checking out the greatest names in your industry. These organisations probably have retail facades in essentially every significant city and many states. Research whether these organisations offer business diversifying potential open doors and focus on reaching those that do.

3. Contact promising franchisors: Many organisations work site pages completely committed to their diversifying open doors. Find these internet based assets and use them to get more data and contact the establishments that interest you. Odds are you'll hear back in the span of 24 hours and get the chance to plan a call - take it. On the off chance that you get an answer long following 24 hours, you might pass better, seeking after different establishments.

4. Pose inquiries during your underlying franchisor call: During your planned call, get some information about the states where the franchisor is looking for franchisees and how fruitful other franchisees have been. Think about this call a low-stakes starting conversation - you're simply attempting to comprehend diversifying rudiments and decide whether the establishment seems OK for you. Recollect that the individual you're chatting with is likewise on a reality tracking down mission. Maybe they need franchisees to have explicit industry experience. They might need franchisees to have essential business ability and an enterprising drive to succeed. Numerous franchisors and franchisees who comprehend advertising, client care and deals - and are worried about expanding exchanges. Decide whether your business experience and enterprising thoughts fit the franchisor's vision of promising franchisees.

5. Visit franchising areas: Subsequent to pinpointing a promising establishment opportunity, visit establishment customer facing facades in various districts to check whether their marking and tasks are predictable across areas. See all clients confronting representatives to affirm that they treat clients suitably. Be certain all areas you visit are perfect and efficient. These are signs that your potential franchisor really puts resources into its franchisees.

6. Get input from current franchisees: The most effective way to find out about an establishment is to talk straightforwardly to involved members. Get some information about the franchisor's emotionally supportive network, permitting charges and any eliteness it offers inside a particular Postal division or span from a specific area. A few establishments hold a "disclosure day" or comparable occasions where you can address delegates and become familiar with diversifying open doors. Additionally, going to diverse industry meetings, for example, the Global franchise Affiliation's yearly gathering, is a great method for recognizing and looking at choices.

7. Ask about and include all potential franchise beginning expenses:

All that you've gained from conversing with current franchisees and the franchisor could advise you that beginning an establishment is costly. You can truly get a feeling of the numbers with an Franchise Exposure Report (FDD). Here, you'll see your sovereignties, franchise expenses, expected instalments to compulsory merchants and brand reserves. Past these expenses, consider the expense of any gear you'll require and any showcasing efforts you'll embrace. There are likewise work out expenses and permits to operate to consider, also paying representatives. You'll confront less monetary difficulties in the event that you meet the franchisor's fluid capital and total assets necessities. You ought to likewise assess progressing costs, for example, the expense of acquiring the products you'll utilise or sell. Franchisors frequently require franchisees to utilise a foreordained arrangement of sellers with preset markups on their deal costs. The last option might build your buying costs. As you research these continuous expenses, audit your FDD to see the franchisor's case and liquidation history. Doing so can see any difficulties you could face in working in your area.

8. Utilise the FDD to track down the franchisor's number of open and shut down areas and the purposes for the terminations: Consider contacting withdrew franchisees for significant criticism to supplement the editorial you've previously gotten.

9. Survey the franchisor's Thing Much of the time: Franchisors will give you a conventional Thing record framing your likely deals, income and benefit. Survey this report and affirm that there are numerous areas, both claimed and diversified, in the exhibition estimations. Pose inquiries in light of these numbers. In the event that your franchisor declines to share a Thing 19, inquire as to why.

10. Think about your establishment domains and backing: Your diversifying understanding ought to give your customer facing facade select working privileges inside a particular area. Search for such language in your agreement, and ask with your franchisor about any worries.

Also, survey your agreement to comprehend the degree of preparing you'll get toward the beginning and franchisor support from there on. You ought to be sure that you have the franchisor's full sponsorship constantly.

11. Settle on your diversifying choice: Since franchisors will frequently get you into a 10-year contract, you ought to ponder the excursion you embraced to pick this establishment. Did you feel happy with asking the franchisor inquiries? Were there yellow or warnings en route? Is there a reasonable chance to bring in significant cash? On the off chance that you feel you're in a decent spot, follow your impulses and sign the agreement.

CHAPTER 5

Stages Of Franchise Growth

In the same way as other organisations, a franchisee will commonly encounter four particular stages during its lifetime: fire up, development, undertaking and restoration or decline. Each stage will introduce its own remarkable provokes and open doors to the entrepreneur, there are a few patterns which are normal to all franchisees.

1. The starting up stage

Despite the fact that getting involved with an establishment mitigates a ton of the gamble related with beginning another business, the beginning up stage can in any case be weighed down with possible entanglements for the franchisee.

During this beginning phase, entrepreneurs should ride horde disciplines, from organisation and bookkeeping to promoting and HR. This can be intellectually wearing and tedious - you'll feel like you're quickly turning many plates more often than not!

Having heaps of capital during this stage is likewise fundamental as it regularly requires as long as three years for new companies to make money. Consequently it is crucial to guarantee income is kept positive and bankruptcy is forestalled.

In any case, as referenced, a colossal benefit of diversifying during the beginning up stage is that you'll approach direction and backing from the franchisor, as well as other franchisees in the organisation, to control you in the correct bearing. Ensure you exploit their help however much as could be expected in the event that you at any point feel overwhelmed. You'll likewise have the advantage of a laid out brand name and a business framework that is demonstrated to be productive.

Despite the fact that it tends to be not difficult to get deterred at introductory mishaps during the beginning up stage, recall that all fruitful establishment proprietors will have encountered comparative disappointments prior to making progress. On the off chance that they can make it happen, so can you.

2. The development stage

In spite of the fact that it will differ from one business to another, most establishments will stir things up around town stage around the long term mark. Right now you'll have a consistent progression of clients, income will be reliable and your own pay will be manageable. You'll be beginning to find things moderately agreeable and will normally begin to make back the initial investment and see a profit from your underlying venture.

3. The development stage

In spite of the fact that it will differ from one business to another, most establishments will stir things up around town stage around the long term mark. Right now you'll have a consistent progression of clients, income will be reliable and your own pay will be manageable. You'll be beginning to find things moderately agreeable and will normally begin to make back the initial investment and see a profit from your underlying venture. The development stage will frequently be the point at which you make a stride back from the everyday running of your business and representative administration obligations to your staff. It's basic to amplify the assets you have within reach as this will empower you to zero in on the master plan and think about learning experiences. Is now the right time to put resources into more stock? Do you have to enlist more staff to deal with requests? Would it be advisable for you to put more into deals and showcasing? The response could be some or the entirety of the abovementioned. While considering development plans, attempt to define Shrewd objectives (explicit, quantifiable, feasible, pertinent, and time-bound) that give clear bearing on the most proficient method to accomplish your development targets. Albeit most parts of your business will turn out to be more agreeable in the development stage, you really must keep an idea about income. In any event, for effective business bankruptcy can immediately turn into a chance on the off chance that neglected solicitations gather.

3. The venture/development stage

Following quite a long while of running your establishment you'll arrive at the undertaking (or development) stage. This is when income is solid and income is sufficiently high to guarantee that all expenses are covered and you are creating a decent gain. During the venture stage some franchisees will try and start to venture into new units and domains.

It may very well be not difficult to become open during the endeavour stage so you should n't nod off at the worst possible time and permit your business to move away from its crowd base.

4. The recharging or decline stage

All longstanding franchising organisations will definitely arrive at the last phase of the franchise lifecycle. How they handle it will characterise whether they disappear or turn into a persevering through market presence.

Fall in client interest during this stage, the business administration should consistently look for new business potential open doors and it is normal for expenses to be sliced and spending plans fixed to support income. At this crossroads, as a franchise proprietor you should ask yourself: is now the right time to sell or reinvest? In the event that you choose to keep, having the support of a franchisor who is in the know regarding market patterns will presumably help.

CHAPTER 6

How Small Businesses Can Grow Through Franchising

As a laid out business procedure, franchising can assist you with taking advantage of a specific hole in the market before any possible contenders.

In a commonplace diversifying understanding, you permit different organisations to sell your administrations or items under your image. You permit them to utilise your intellectual Property (IP), including exchange stamps, copyright and skill, as well as your plan of action. Once the franchisee has set up their business, you furnish them with progressing support.

Consequently, the franchisee pays you an underlying charge, trailed by eminences - commonly a level of the deals or benefits. You may likewise create a pay from the increase on any items and administrations that you offer to your franchisees.

One more advantage of franchising is diminished gamble. The franchisees bear the expenses and the dangers of the business, and you get a surefire charge. Additionally, on the grounds that the franchisees are maintaining their own organisations, you benefit from restricting your own administration expenses or you might decide to charge the franchisees for your mastery.

Franchising your business can be a distinct advantage for making quick development and progress. By utilising the enterprising soul and drive of franchisees, you can fabricate an organisation of enthusiastic people who put resources into the outcome of your image.

Nonetheless, it's vital that franchising is certainly not a dependable way to progress. It requires cautious preparation, exhaustive exploration, and progressing backing to guarantee that both you and your franchisees thrive.

At last, franchising is an organisation, and correspondence and joint effort are urgent. Remain associated with your franchisees, pay attention to their input, and offer the fundamental help and assets they need. Support a feeling of local area inside your establishment organisation and enable your franchisees to succeed.

Franchising can be an interesting and remunerating venture whenever drawn nearer with tirelessness and devotion. In this way, on the off chance that you're prepared to take your business higher than ever, consider diversifying as an incredible asset for development and achievement.

CONCLUSION

The franchising model offers a remarkable road for development, permitting business visionaries to use the strength of their image, benefit from nearby market experiences, and offer the dangers and obligations with persuaded franchisees.

One key focus point is the principal significance of a clear cut and replicable plan of action. Franchise achievement depends on the capacity to make a framework that can be effectively copied without forfeiting quality or consistency. This includes classifying functional cycles, laying out far reaching preparing projects, and cultivating a culture that resounds across all franchise areas.

Additionally, viable correspondence and coordinated effort with franchisees are fundamental. Building solid connections, offering continuous help, and encouraging a feeling of local area among franchisees add to a strong and joined brand character. Customary criticism channels, open lines of correspondence, and a pledge to shared accomplishment establish a positive climate where both franchisor and franchisee flourish.

In the always advancing scene of business, versatility is critical.

Adaptability in answering business sector patterns, purchaser inclinations, and mechanical progressions guarantees the progress with importance and seriousness of the establishment model. Monetary reasonability couldn't possibly be more significant. Franchise improvement requires a sensible way to deal with capital designation, adjusting the interest in extension with the requirement for keeping up with monetary security.

A very much organised monetary model, straightforward monetary detailing, and a sensible comprehension of the underlying and continuous expenses related with franchising are basic to long haul achievement. At last, the progress of a franchising framework is inherently attached to the outcome of its singular units. Perceiving the special necessities of different business sectors, engaging franchisees with independence inside the structure of the brand, and cultivating a cooperative climate improve the aggregate strength of the franchise framework. By encouraging a vigorous plan of action, keeping up with compelling correspondence, embracing versatility, and practising monetary judiciousness, business visionaries can open the maximum capacity of their image. In doing so, they extend their business impression as well as add to the achievement and flourishing of the franchisees who share in the vision of development and greatness.

www.ingramcontent.com/pod-product-compliance
Lightning Source LLC
Chambersburg PA
CBHW071001290526
45795CB00005B/1735